MARILYN HICKEY MINISTRIES

God's Plan
for
Abundance

What? Why? How?

MARILYN HICKEY

God's Plan for Abundance: What? Why? How?

Marilyn Hickey Ministries
PO Box 6598
Englewood, CO 80155-6598
marilynandsarah.org

ISBN - 978-1-938696-25-1

Printed in the United States of America.

CONTENTS

1

LIVING AN ABUNDANT LIFE

Jesus came to give us an abundant life. So, what does an abundant life look like? Scripture gives us insight into how His redemption plan not only provides for our salvation, but it is also God's plan for abundance. His plan covers all facets of our lives. His plan counteracts all the wicked, evil schemes that the devil has devised against us: *"The thief does not come except to steal, and to kill, and to destroy. I have come that they may have life, and that they may have it more abundantly"* (John 10:10).

His plan provides for an abundance of peace (see Psalm 37:11) and having plenty to eat and drink: *"Everyone who thirsts, come to the waters; and you who have no money, come, buy and eat. Yes, come, buy wine and milk without money and without price"* (Isaiah 55:1). We can see that abundance illustrated when the Israelites were in the wilderness, desperately looking for water. God *"split the rocks in the wilderness, and gave them drink in abundance like the depths"* (Psalm 78:15).

His plan is also designed to meet all your needs, from finances to health. One of the most profound truths of the Bible is that God wants His children to prosper: *"Beloved, I pray that you may prosper in all things..."* (3 John v. 2). God calls you "beloved." So, if you are born again, are you beloved? Yes! He is telling you, His beloved, that He loves you so much, and He wants more than anything else that you might abound in all areas of your life, even financially. Your abundance is His will for you.

We must understand that we have a heavenly Father who is not looking at us to beat us up. He is looking at us, of course, but that's in order to change us and to make us more like Him. And He's looking at us to bless us. He wants us to abound in all things: *"You crown the year with Your goodness, and Your paths drip with abundance"* (Psalm 65:11). Yet, many Christians are floundering. Though they are saved, they don't understand why some folks are blessed, and they're not; they don't know how to achieve that abundance. It may be because they are not thoroughly sold out to this truth, thoroughly convinced, that God wants them to "drip with abundance"! If you're not convinced, you're not going to have faith to believe for an abundant life to do what God wants you to do. I think sometimes we haven't stood in faith like we need to and claimed what belongs to us.

We must know that we know that we know, that abundance is the will of God for us. It is God's will because He loves us. Point to yourself. Say, "God loves me, just like I am, sweet or ugly. He still loves me." God doesn't play favorites. He doesn't love you more than He loves me. We are all equal in His eyes because we are all made in His image.

A caveat I must point out is that I personally must live the way God tells me to live in order to teach you what He tells me to teach you about His plan for abundance. It's connected to the anointing. If I don't live it, the anointing doesn't come on you. It would be like a financial whiz telling people how to get rich while he's embezzling funds from his company, or if somebody taught you how to live a holy life while they were living in fornication. Sadly, I've seen this happen in churches where leadership was living an immoral lifestyle, and nobody knew about it. Pretty soon, all the people were involved in immorality because the thing that was on the head came on the body. I want you to know there is an anointing on this ministry for abundance because we are conforming to what God tells us to do, and we are transforming our minds.

The Key to Abundance is in You

I can't say it enough—God wants you to have an abundant life! He wants *"your soul* [to] *delight itself in abundance"* (Isaiah 55:2). In order to let this truth sink in, we must take a look at the principles God has set down regarding His plan. We will also see that if we break them and try to live according to our own rules, it is not going to work.

If we look again at 3 John v. 2, the first principle is soul prosperity: *"Beloved, I pray that you may prosper in all things and be in health, **just as your soul prospers**"* (emphasis added). It begins with the salvation of your soul; then God's plan for abundance can unfold in your life. It doesn't depend on your boss. It's not your mother-in-law leaving you a house. It's not your wife getting a better job or your husband getting a promotion. Your key to abundance is in you. I will say it again: You don't have to make God want to bless you. He already does!

You must see and believe that God wants to bless you! Look at the patriarchs and matriarchs of the Old Testament. Was Abraham born wealthy? What about Job, Esther, Joseph, and David? Even Job, who lost everything but his nagging wife, gained back twice what he had lost. They all started with little or nothing (especially in David's case). Yet all of them were living according to God's principles, and God blessed them—abundantly blessed them! They didn't follow the world's principles. They followed God's. We all must live in the world, but we don't have to act like the world. Job 36:11 says:

> *If they obey and serve Him,*
> *They shall spend their days in prosperity,*
> *And their years in pleasures.*

That leads us to the second principle: We must not conform to the world's standard of thinking about materialism. We must be transformed by God's standard. You have to get your head going in another direction. If we don't say what the Lord says and instead follow the ways of the world, it is possible to end up like the Israelites did after they had been in the promised land for a while. The world's ways had become their ways. When they did what they saw the world around them doing and failed to heed the warnings of the prophets God sent to them again and again, they were exiled from the land God had given them. God warned them again and again. Finally, He had no other recourse but to deal with them according to the Word He had sent them:

> *"Just as the Lord of hosts determined to do to us,*
> *According to our ways and according to our deeds,*
> *So He has dealt with us."* (Zechariah 1:6)

The world says, "Get all you can and can all you get," and "He who dies with the most toys wins." But guess what? He still dies, so that is not a good goal. Even if you die a millionaire, who is going to spend it? You're not. You're dead!

In Luke 12:16-21, Jesus told a parable about this. A rich man had such a good harvest that he thought he could take it easy:

> I will say to my soul, "Soul, you have many goods laid up for many years; take your ease; eat, drink, and be merry." But God said to him, "Fool! This night your soul will be required of you; then whose will those things be which you have provided?"
>
> "So is he who lays up treasure for himself, and is not rich toward God."

Your soul must be rich toward God and not focused on how much you can get. How do you do that? Romans 12:2 says: *"And do not be conformed to this world, but be transformed by the renewing of your mind, that you may prove what is that good and acceptable and perfect will of God."* To be transformed, you have to renew your mind. The best way I know to renew your mind is to get into the Bible every day. Spend time in the Word. I would even suggest you look up all the references to abundance, prosperity, wealth, rich, debt, and poor. Write down what the Lord shows you about them. Then start putting them into practice.

We cannot be moved by circumstances. We must be moved by the Word: *"In the house of the righteous there is much treasure, but in the revenue of the wicked is trouble"* (Proverbs 15:6). Did you know that money makes trouble for wicked people? Proverbs 1:32 (KJV) tells us, *"The prosperity of fools shall destroy them."* If you look up "prosperity of the wicked" in the Bible, you will find that the wicked have a problem with their wealth. It gets them into crazy lusts and junky things they shouldn't be into. They misuse and abuse money. Money becomes an idol. They go after it, and it really becomes a problem for them; for some, it may lead them to evil. Psalm 52:5, 7 even warns us that God will destroy men who trust in their abundance:

> *God shall . . . destroy you forever;*
> *"Here is the man who did not make God his strength,*
> *But trusted in the abundance of his riches,*
> *And strengthened himself in his wickedness."*

We sometimes read or hear about people who win a $50 million lottery, then you read about them committing suicide, getting divorced, or filing for bankruptcy. Money is not a blessing to those who are worldly. They don't know how to use it correctly. They live by the world's standard that conforms to what the world thinks about money.

Years ago, I found a little poem that speaks to this. I thought it was good because it is about what the dollar bill says to people:

> You hold me in your hand and call me yours,
> Yet may I not as well call you mine?
> See how easily I rule you?
> To gain me, you would all but die.
> I am valuable as rain, essential as water.
> Without me, men and institutions would die.
> Yet I do not hold the power of life for them.
> I am futile without the stamp of your desire.
> I go nowhere unless you send me.
> I keep a strange company.
> For me men make love and scorn character.
> Yet I am appointed to the service of saints,
> To give education to the growing mind

And food to the starving bodies of the poor.

My power is terrific.

Handle me carefully and wisely

Lest you become my servant rather than I being yours.

–Author Unknown

Money, the "what" of the righteous, has a "why." This "why" becomes a blessing to them, and it also blesses others. Then you begin to see that God wants us to be blessed and He has a "why" for that blessing. God also shows us the "how" that goes with it. Money is to be our servant. We are not to be a servant to money. That is conforming to the world's standards instead of being transformed by the Word. That's why we transform our minds.

So, let me pray with you before we go any further. Say, "Father, help me to be transformed, renewed by the Word of God in my mind about money and materialism. Help me today and always. Open my eyes. Let me see. In Jesus's name. Amen."

2

The "What" and "Why" of God's Plan for Abundance

Blessings are upon the righteous because God wants us to live abundant lives. Blessings are the "what" to financial abundance. However, with the "what" that He gives us, He has a "why." God has a reason for blessing us.

Understanding what Jesus says to us is most important. The very last command that Jesus gave us was the crucial one. It's in Matthew 28:19-20:

> *Go therefore and make disciples of all the nations, baptizing*
> *them in the name of the Father and of the Son and of the*
> *Holy Spirit, teaching them to observe all things that I have*
> *commanded you.*

Jesus's first priority was to win the world. His priority must become our priority. We must be concerned about the lost: the lost around us—the lost who are in our city, our state, our nation, and the world.

A while back, some people went out to dinner. One of them, a Christian businessman from our church, said to the waitress, "Now we're going to pray over our food. Is there anything you would like us to pray about for you?" She said, "Yes, there is." She gave him a list of her prayer requests, and they prayed for her. I believe God began to touch her and open her heart. What do you see here? It is someone who cares about souls. It is responding to the Great Commission, making Christ's priority his priority.

Jesus said, *"Seek first the kingdom of God"* (Matthew 6:33). That's souls. To God, there is nothing more important in the world than souls. If we are seeking first the kingdom of God, we are seeking souls. The second part of this verse is that we also seek his righteousness—that's saving souls. We want and need that. The last part of this verse says, *"all these things shall be added to you."* In the world, we are going after things, but a Christian should be going after the kingdom by going after souls and righteous living. Then God will provide the things you need. Hallelujah! When you seek first the kingdom, God is coming along behind you with cars, houses, promotions, and more to meet your needs—in other words, abundance!

Notice you didn't go after them. You went after the kingdom, right? And then what happened? All these things came after you. Wow! God gives you the "what," but with every "what," there is a "why."

Do you know that almost 30 percent of the whole world's wealth is in the United States, though only 4.25 percent of the world's population lives here? Why would God bless us so much? Because he has a "why" that goes with the "what" we have received, and historically, Americans have invested their wealth into the kingdom to seek souls. I believe that Christians and our mission programs are what have kept America afloat. I think that has been a huge factor in America's blessings.

Allow me a soap-box moment here. Currently, our culture appears to be drifting away from Christianity, and a live-and-let-live mentality is gripping the nation in the name of "tolerance." Let me warn you—God has not changed his command to his Church. Millions of people will go to hell because there are Christians who haven't fulfilled the Great Commission. They haven't sown any of the "what" God has given them into His kingdom. They consume it on their own lusts.

A word of caution is needed here, so let's look at this a bit closer. Don't ask God why you are struggling financially if you aren't concerned about souls. Your "what" can deceive you about "why" God has given it to you. We look at the "what" and say, "What? What? I want more! I want more!" Then we begin to focus on what we don't have. Let me tell you, the Chinese people would be thrilled to have our social security! They would think they were millionaires! Don't be deceived! We must realize that the "what" has a "why," and if we will concentrate on the "why," we'll get a lot more "what" to go with it.

Look at the Laodicean church in Revelation 3:16-17:

> *So then, because you are lukewarm, and neither cold nor hot, I will vomit you out of My mouth. Because you say, "I am rich, have become wealthy, and have need of nothing"— and do not know that you are wretched, miserable, poor, blind, and naked.*

This is the church age we live in. You and I both know rich people who are not serving God, and they are miserable. They are wretched. They have the "what," but they don't have the "why." What did Jesus say to this church?

I counsel you to buy from Me gold refined in the fire, that you may be rich; and white garments, that you may be clothed, that the shame of your nakedness may not be revealed; and anoint your eyes with eye salve, that you may see. (Revelation 3:18)

If you have the "what" and you're not looking at the "why," you are blind, you are poor, you are wretched, you are miserable, and you are naked. Even if you're wearing a mink coat, living in Beverly Hills, and driving a Porsche, you are poor because you don't follow up the "what" with the "why." Fortunately, we do have some role models to follow to reverse this. Let's look at some biblical examples.

Esther's "Why"

Esther was an orphan who had been adopted by her cousin. Though she wasn't born into wealth, Esther was loaded because she married the richest man on earth at that time. She was the queen of the Persian kingdom and was tremendously wealthy. Can you imagine the wealth that this woman had? She could go to Nordstrom and say, "I'll take the whole store. I'll take the whole floor of shoes." She could go home with 10,000 pairs of shoes and go back the next day and buy 10,000 more! We look at Esther and are amazed at the amount of "what" God had given her. Talk about abundance! After she came to the throne, we read that God had a "why" for her riches.

So, what was her "why"? Despite her vast wealth, she had a despicable enemy, Haman, a wretch if there ever was one! He had gotten the king to sign a decree to kill all the Jewish people in the kingdom. Guess who was behind that? The devil, of course! Neither Haman nor the king knew that Esther was a Jew. Esther's cousin, Mordecai, found out about his plot and went to Esther. He sent her a message, asking her to go to the king and intercede for her people. She was hesitant to do so, for if the king had not summoned her, she could be killed. But Mordecai pressed her:

> *"Do not think in your heart that you will escape in the king's palace any more than all the other Jews. For if you remain completely silent at this time, relief and deliverance will arise for the Jews from another place, but you and your father's house will perish. Yet who knows whether you have come to the kingdom for such a time as this?"* (Esther 4:13-14)

There's an important key here. If you don't put the kingdom first, God is not going to lose. He will just get somebody else. Who is the loser? Not God. You are the loser. I don't want to be the loser. I don't want God to raise up somebody else in my place. I want to do what God called me to do, and I'm sure you do, too. Plus, do you really want to risk being destroyed? Mordecai told Esther that if she didn't go to the king, somebody else would—and she could be destroyed. If you feel you are to do something, consider this: could you have been called for "such a time as this"?

There was no question, she was called, and her "what" had a "why." She agreed to go to the king with a condition—that the Jews pray and fast with her.

> *"Go, gather all the Jews who are present in Shushan, and fast for me; neither eat nor drink for three days, night or day. My maids and I will fast likewise. And so I will go to the king, which is against the law; and if I perish, I perish!"* (Esther 4:16)

Despite the threat to her life, she would disobey man's law—in this case, the king's law—to fulfill God's will. She would go to the king, saying, "If I perish, I perish." Now, her money could have destroyed her; her wealth and her position could have destroyed her. She could have said, "Hey, I'm not going in there. Nobody knows I'm a Jewess. I'm not doing it. I'm not going to lose these 10,000 pairs of shoes! I'm not going to go in there. No way." Her wealth could have been a deterrent, for that very wealth—the "what" she had—could have destroyed her.

Instead, she focused on "why." She put the kingdom first. Her cousin's words must have been ringing in her ears: *"Who knows whether you have come to the kingdom for such a time as this?"* Folks, we were born at this time, the end of the ages, for such a time as this. Why? Is it just for us to have a new house? A new car? God's not against those things. Those are good things. But our money could go to win souls, especially as we see the end is near and time is short. What are we here for? Just to look good? Smell good? No, our "why" is the kingdom!

What did Esther do next? Well, she got all dressed up because she had someplace to go! Now America is all dressed up. We have some places to go. We have to go and take the gospel to people who would otherwise never hear; and if you're not going, then you need to be sending the goers! Support your church's missionaries or other mission endeavors. It is so important that you get ahold of the "why"! There's a "why" for your life. Now you may say, "Well, I was an accident." No, you weren't! You have a divine destiny with God. Everybody has a divine destiny with God. Don't ever tell me you're an accident! That's not biblical.

When Esther arrived at the king's court, he granted her favor, and she invited the king and Haman to a meal she would specially prepare. The king and Haman accepted the invitation. When they arrived, the king was curious as to what she wanted. He even offered her half of the kingdom. She was wise though not to act too hastily. She responded that she would tell him the next day at another banquet she would prepare for them. At that point, her "why" would be revealed.

Her "why" was the salvation of her people. The following day, she explained to the king that Haman's edict meant he wanted to kill both her and her people. The king became enraged, stalked off, and when he came back, ordered the execution of Haman—on the very gallows that Haman had ordered be built to hang Mordecai. Because Esther found the courage to stand for her people, the king allowed letters to be sent to everyone in his kingdom, allowing the Jews to defend themselves and survive.

> The Jews gathered together in their cities throughout all the provinces of King Ahasuerus to lay hands on those who sought their harm. And no one could withstand them, because fear of them fell upon all people. (Esther 9:2)

What would you have done in Esther's shoes? Would you have the courage to take a stand against evil plots to destroy God's people? Christians all around the world are being persecuted for their faith. Some are standing strong, refusing to bend their knee to anyone but their Lord and Savior—and being killed as a result. Look at what is happening in Sudan, Nigeria, China, and North Korea. Could your "why" be something as simple as praying for these faithful Christians?

You see, when God created you and filled you with His Spirit, there was a "why" for you. You're not just filled with the Holy Spirit to speak in tongues, get inspiration, and all those wonderful gifts you get from Him. Jesus said that when the Holy Spirit came upon us, we would be his witnesses:

> "But you shall receive power when the Holy Spirit has come upon you; and you shall be witnesses to Me in Jerusalem, and in all Judea and Samaria, and to the end of the earth." (Acts 1:8)

The "why" of the Holy Spirit is the kingdom! God saved you, and His "why" was to get you to win the lost and get you interested in the kingdom. And, as we have already seen, if you'll put the kingdom first, God will provide for your needs.

The Lepers' "Why"

When I think of lepers, especially in Bible times, I don't particularly feel that they were able to contribute much. Most of them had almost nothing. Leprosy was an ugly thing; lepers were missing eyes, a nose, a big toe, or a thumb. Lepers were ostracized from society and placed under a 24/7 quarantine for the rest of their lives. In 2 Kings 7, we read that they are starving to death, along with all of Samaria.

Samaria was being attacked by Syria, and it was a terrible, awful time. The lepers were outside the city gates (apparently, they weren't allowed in) when they made a decision that would affect the outcome of the war.

> There were four leprous men at the entrance of the gate; and they said to one another, "Why are we sitting here until we die? If we say, 'We will enter the city,' the famine is in the city, and we shall die there. And if we sit here, we die also. Now, therefore, come, let us surrender to the army of the Syrians. If they keep us alive, we shall live; and if they kill us, we shall only die." (2 Kings 7:3-4)

They were hoping the Syrians would show them mercy and feed them. They probably thought the Syrians would look at their missing ears, noses, hands and take pity on them. So, they went out to the Syrian camp thinking, *Whether we die here or die there, it can't hurt.* Let's face it. They had nothing to offer—they had no "what"—or so it seemed.

What they didn't know was that God had sent the sound of an army ahead of them, not an actual army, but the sound of an army. When the Syrians heard the sound of this army, they fled and left all of their wealth—they had a lot of money, and a lot of food. But the lepers didn't know that. The lepers only dared to approach the enemy's camp, and when they did, they were in for a surprise. Nobody was there, but lots of things were:

> *And when these lepers came to the outskirts of the camp,*
> *they went into one tent and ate and drank, and carried from*
> *it silver and gold and clothing, and went and hid them; then*
> *they came back and entered another tent, and carried some*
> *from there also, and went and hid it.* (2 Kings 7:8)

Suddenly they were wealthy! They had a "what" to fulfill God's "why" for their lives. There were clothes, gold, silver, horses, food, and more that the Syrians had left behind in their haste to escape what they thought was an approaching army. In their sudden joy, they realized that there was more than enough to bring relief to their countrymen—in other words, abundance. They decided to let the king know. In the midst of their "what," they got ahold of the "why," and they went and shared the good news.

The lepers gave of the "what" they now had. If you remember, the people all rushed out there; the famine was over. There was enough to feed the people, and it broke the whole pattern of poverty. The lepers found their purpose, and their "why" saved their people.

Who knows? If you're seeking the kingdom first and putting God first, could it break the poverty in a whole lot of areas in other people's lives? I've noticed that there's something about people when they begin to be transformed by the Word, renewed by the Word, and obey the Word—they're contagious. They begin to have the smell of victory. God's plan for abundance is fulfilled in the lives of people who tithe, sow offerings, love souls, and put the kingdom first.

The Israelites' "Why"

Those lepers saved a city from starvation. Esther saved her nation from being totally annihilated. Now let's go on to the Israelites. Let's look at them because, as you will see, when they begin to see the "why," it's out of this world.

> Now the children of Israel had done according to the word of Moses, and they had asked from the Egyptians articles of silver, articles of gold, and clothing. And the Lord had given the people favor in the sight of the Egyptians, so that they granted them what they requested. Thus they plundered the Egyptians. (Exodus 12:35-36)

"Now, wait a minute," you might ask, "was there a 'why' to that wealth?" Think about it: they have all this money, and they're going into the wilderness. How are they going to buy anything out in the wilderness? There is no grocery store. There is no shoe store. There's no cart and buggy store. There's nothing in the wilderness! They are loaded with money and wealth and have no place to spend it. So, if God has a "what," does He have a "why"? Of course He does!

The Israelites were in the midst of the wilderness when God told Moses to have them *"make Me a sanctuary, that I may dwell among them"* (Exodus 25:8). They had the linen, gold, silver, brass, and the jewels they had taken from Egypt. God asked for their tithes and offerings because He wanted a sanctuary. If you think, "Well, they built a church," then you don't get it. It wasn't just a church. They built a place where God's presence would come and dwell with them. They readily agreed because they wanted the presence of God to dwell with them!

What do you want in your life? What do I want in my life? The same thing the Israelites wanted: the presence of God in our lives. Matthew 6:21 says, *"For where your treasure is, there your heart will be also."* If your treasure goes where God's kingdom is, where God's heart is, you know that God's heart is going to come into your situation. God's heart and God's presence will come into your treasure when you go after His presence.

The Israelites had seen the pillar of cloud and the pillar of fire, but how many of you know it's better to feel His presence and have His presence dwell among you? And so, when they built the tabernacle and the holy of holies over the ark of the covenant, the presence of God came down. Hallelujah! The "why" of their "what" was to bring the presence of God into their lives.

Let me tell you, people do not understand that when they don't tithe, and they don't sow offerings, they can lose out on the presence of God. Maybe you don't believe that. You might think I'm crazy, but honey, it's in the Bible! You'll have to go through your Bible and rip those pages out and say, "God is wrong," if that's what you think!

Joseph's "Why"

Joseph is a great example for people who might think that nothing ever works out for them and those who feel abused and even abandoned. He lost his home and family, well, not really "lost." He was sold into slavery by his brothers. Despite the harsh treatment by his brothers, once he was settled into a new household, *"Joseph found favor in [Potiphar's] sight, and served him. Then [Potiphar] made him overseer of his house, and all that he had he put under his authority"* (Genesis 39:4).

Potiphar was blessed because Joseph was there. Joseph worked hard and did his best in a difficult situation. When he was tempted by Potiphar's wife, he could have lost his righteousness, but he did not get involved with her. He sought first the kingdom and God's righteousness. The implications here are that you can't live any old way and say, "Well, I tithe. So what if we're not married and living together? That's okay." Folks, find that for me in the Bible! It's not righteousness, and God's plan for abundance is not going to work for you with that kind of lifestyle.

Joseph kept the kingdom first. Potiphar's wife falsely accused Joseph of trying to rape her, and as a result, Potiphar threw him into prison. Even in prison, God never deserted Joseph:

> But the Lord was with Joseph and showed him mercy, and He gave him favor in the sight of the keeper of the prison. And the keeper of the prison committed to Joseph's hand all the prisoners who were in the prison; whatever they did there, it was his doing. The keeper of the prison did not look into anything that was under Joseph's authority, because the Lord was with him; and whatever he did, the Lord made it prosper. (Genesis 39:21-23)

What did the Lord do for Joseph? Verse 23 says He prospered him!

Joseph prospered in Potiphar's household. He prospered in prison. But who wants to stay in prison? Finally, there came a day when everything changed for him. He was taken from a prison and put into a palace. And it was all because God gave him the interpretation of Pharaoh's dreams of seven years of famine that would follow seven years of abundance. Now he has everything. He's the prime minister. When he drives by in the latest chariot, everybody bows down. They say, "Oh, there's Joseph, the prime minister, the man who saved us."

But God didn't give him the "what" so he could have the latest chariot. God gave him that "what" with a "why." If you're seeking first the kingdom, what is God going to give you? But just remember the "what" has a "why" and it is for kingdom living.

Once the famine hits, it affects his family starving back in Canaan. They are in a very bad way. The brothers end up going to Egypt to buy food, and as a result, they end up meeting with Joseph, who didn't hold any grudges; rather, he gives them food and eventually a new home in Egypt with him. He was able to save his entire family when over 70 members of his family moved down to Egypt. He was such a godly man, so much so that when he revealed himself to his brothers, he said, *"Do not therefore be grieved or angry with yourselves because you sold me here; for God sent me before you to preserve life"* (Genesis 45:5).

There was no vengeance or malice toward his brothers. He obviously understood the "why" of all that had happened to him. And we also see that God's promise in Psalm 5:12 is so applicable to it: *"For you bless the godly, O Lord; you surround them with your shield of love"* (NLT). Joseph didn't become bitter and turn against his brothers. He was a godly man, and God really did surround him with a shield of love that protected him from falling into the trap of vengeance. There was no malice toward his brothers; he loved his brothers.

What was the "why"? The "why" wasn't to ride in a golden chariot or to have all the wealth and say, "Notice me, look at me." Rather, he was there in Egypt ahead of his family to save them—the beginnings of God's chosen people through whom the Messiah would come. Joseph's "why" helped to guarantee our salvation, and because of that, we can see God's plan through it all.

Folks, who knows what will happen when you sow your treasure into the kingdom? What is it going to do? Who will come into the kingdom because of your gifts? Could it be the next Billy Graham or Oral Roberts? Maybe Amy Carmichael or Hudson Taylor? Could it be another great apologist or theologian like Paul who can effectively communicate the gospel to an often-hostile world? Why? Because God has a "why" that goes with all the "what" that He gives us.

Marilyn Hickey Ministries exists because God called me to "cover the earth with the Word." On my own, I could never dream of what God has used me to accomplish. It is only through the faithful giving of thousands of people all over the world who sow into this ministry. They are the people who make it possible to broadcast the gospel into closed countries. People who have given their "what" have enabled my team and me to hold healing meetings in many countries, even Muslim countries. These givers made it possible for me to minister to a million Muslims in Pakistan in just one meeting. The "what" of generous partners has given God the open doors to show off. As a result, the blind have gained their sight; the lame have walked; growths, tumors, and warts have disappeared. And, most importantly, countless individuals have been born again. Many of them are now serving the Lord in ministry around the world. It's all because people trusted God and used the "what" He gave them to bring about all these "whys."

3

THE "HOW" OF ABUNDANCE

If we are not thriving in God's plan of abundance, nothing is wrong with God. Something is wrong with us. A big part of the "how" in God's plan is to figure out what's wrong and what's not working. We have been programmed by the world to see that the "how" to abundance comes from a job, an inheritance, or a surprise win in some contest. By now, though, you should realize that God's ways are not the world's ways.

Examine your heart, lifestyle, and motives. What doesn't line up with the Word? Do a checkup to discover how to reverse that and make sure you are not doing something to hinder God's plan working in your life. Then get into agreement with God because when you get in agreement with Him, that's when things begin to happen.

Checkup! What's Wrong? – The Love of Money

Proverbs 11:8-9 says:

> *The righteous is delivered from trouble,*
> *And it comes to the wicked instead.*
> *The hypocrite with his mouth destroys his neighbor,*
> *But through knowledge the righteous will be delivered.*

We can be delivered from debt. We can be delivered from poverty, from lack. We can be delivered from the lust of money. You have probably heard this saying over and over: "Money talks." Money does talk. Earlier, we saw that money talks and says a lot of things, but folks, we shouldn't be listening to money talking. We should be listening to God talking and then let the money follow.

When I think about how listening to money affects us, I think about Balaam and it's very sad. He was into witchcraft, and people would go to him to have him seek the will of God through demons. Nowadays, it's like calling the psychic hotline or going to a fortune teller. Balaam was a false prophet, and the devil came after him, not with money, but with the love of money. First Timothy 6:10 warns us of this: *"For the love of money is a root of all kinds of evil, for which some have strayed from the faith in their greediness, and pierced themselves through with many sorrows."*

The love of money led to Balaam's downfall. Balak, king of Moab, sent for Balaam to come and curse the Israelites who were camped in the plains of Moab on their trek to the promised land. He enticed Balaam by offering him a lot of money. God warned him several different times not to go, and at first Balaam was reluctant to go. However, eventually, he went. He never did curse the Israelites, because God said, "You can't curse what I have blessed." In the end, assuming he didn't repent, he lost his soul because of his lust for money.

The "how" to abundance in this case is, "Don't let money talk to you! Let God talk to you." How does God talk to you? Mostly through the Bible. It has everything to do with not being conformed to the world.

Checkup! What's Wrong? – Conformity to the World

Romans 12:2 tells us not to be conformed to the world. The New Living Translation elaborates even further:

> Don't copy the behavior and customs of this world, but let God transform you into a new person by changing the way you think. Then you will learn to know God's will for you, which is good and pleasing and perfect.

I've said it before, and I'll say it again: keep your mind transformed by the Word of God. In fact, you must study the Word, not just read it, to really allow it to transform you: *"Study and do your best to present yourself to God approved, a workman [tested by trial] who has no reason to be ashamed, accurately handling and skillfully teaching the word of truth"* (2 Timothy 2:15 AMP).

"Study" in this verse means "to exert one's self, endeavor, give diligence." In other words, it is a labor to do this. If you want to know about abundance, study about it. Go through the Bible. Every time you find a Scripture relating to abundance, write it down in a journal (or on your computer) until you have a whole notebook of how much God wants to make you abound. The Bible reveals God's plan of abundance. Don't listen to money talk. Get what God is saying. Then you can build your faith to release what God has for you, which is probably far more than you can imagine. Yes, it's a labor to do this; Yes, it will take time to make a notebook on abundance. Yet you are not just studying all that Word—you are hoarding it!

You are putting the Word inside yourself. You are laying it up as truth to live by. Psalm 51:6 tells us: *"You [God] desire truth in the inward parts, and in the hidden part You will make me to know wisdom."* God is not looking for the Bible on your coffee table or on your computer. He's looking to find it in you! Then He can take that truth that's been stored up, bring it to your mind, and make it wisdom for what you need and what you need to do. Biblical truth will become wisdom to know how to fulfill God's plan for abundance and how to handle abundance in a godly way. The Word not only changes you, but it also conforms you to the kingdom of God.

Now don't be shocked by what I'm about to say. Do you know what biblical abundance really is? I think it's conforming to God by allowing the Word to transform you. The transformation starts in your mind. You may say, "Yeah, but sometimes bad news comes." Psalm 112:6-8 is a powerful reminder that abundance includes peace:

> *Surely he will never be shaken;*
> *The righteous will be in everlasting remembrance.*
> *He will not be afraid of evil tidings;*
> *His heart is steadfast, trusting in the Lord.*
> *His heart is established;*
> *He will not be afraid,*
> *Until he sees his desire upon his enemies.*

God wants to change us. He wants to transform us. The primary "how" is to be transformed by the Word of God. Let it clean you up from the inside out because Jesus desires his Church to be pure and spotless: *"Christ also loved the church and gave Himself for her, that He might sanctify and cleanse her with the washing of water by the word"* (Ephesians 5:25-26). The Word will wash away the world's dirt and its corrupt thinking and prepare you to receive God's blessings.

Say what the Word says, not just about money, but about your life. That's a "how" to biblical abundance. Speak what the Word says about your circumstances, and don't give up! I've noticed the hardest confession is when you're almost ready to get it, but then you think, God, where is it? You can't act like that! Don't let doubt creep in! Instead, thank God that He blesses you with all spiritual blessings in heavenly places (see Ephesians 1:3). Thank God you seek first the kingdom and expect all these things to be added to you (see Matthew 6:33).

Checkup! What's Wrong? – The Devourer

When God blesses them, some people will say, "Oh, I've been waiting for this blessing. I just got a $25,000 bonus! I've been wanting that new car. I'm going to go buy it; this is it." And they go buy the new car. What did they do? They ate (devoured) all their seed. They didn't tithe $2,500 or give $500 for a mission offering. They ate their seed! Folks, if you eat your seed, how are you going to have a harvest? You may want another car next year for your wife, but you ate it all. Poor thing! She didn't get one because you ate so much. Heed the words of 2 Corinthians 9:6-8 because these words are powerful!

> *He who sows sparingly will also reap sparingly, and he who sows bountifully will also reap bountifully. So let each one give as he purposes in his heart, not grudgingly or of necessity; for God loves a cheerful giver. And God is able to make all grace abound toward you, that you, always having all sufficiency in all things, may have an abundance for every good work.*

If you are having a financial problem or lots of them, ask yourself what kind of financial seeds you are sowing. Have you sown sparingly or bountifully? Have you sown just barely? You know, if you sow two carrot seeds, what are you going to get? Two carrots. Other seeds produce differently, like corn which produces multiples, but you don't get that with carrots. Two carrots are all you are going to get. Think about your sowing. What are you sowing? Where are you sowing?

This all leads up to the next "how"—tithing. When you don't tithe, the devil walks right in and takes what little you may have. The devil is also subtle and wants to make people think that tithing is not for today because tithing is of the law. It's imperative that you discover what the Bible says because, as we have seen, we want our knowledge to be transformed as well. We must see what the Word says.

God spoke to Moses and gave him the law of tithing. (So, yes, you are absolutely right; that's Old Testament.) It was in the law, but Abraham was the first tither, and he was some 400 years before Moses. He was tithing 400 years before the law was ever written (see Genesis 14:20). Now let me ask you, have you ever said, "I am the seed of Abraham, and his blessings fall on me"? So, if you are the seed of Abraham, what should you be doing? If you want the blessings of Abraham, how do you get them? How did Abraham get them? Tithing!

Let's see what the New Testament says. Paul wrote: *"On the first day of the week let each one of you lay something aside, storing up as he may prosper, that there be no collections when I come"* (1 Corinthians 16:2). In addition, Jesus taught tithing in Matthew 23:23:

> *"Woe to you, scribes and Pharisees, hypocrites! For you pay tithe of mint and anise and cummin, and have neglected the*

weightier matters of the law: justice and mercy and faith.
These you ought to have done, without leaving the others
undone."

Jesus grouped tithing in with the other "weightier matters of the law," implying that tithing was still part of the law, just like justice, mercy, and faith. You can't ignore it any more than you can those "weightier" laws.

Tithing is both a command and a promise. When you tithe and give offerings, God closes the doors to the enemy. That's the promise; in fact, it is the only promise in which God said He would rebuke the devil for you. Every place else, God tells you to rebuke the devil. If you are a tither, then God will rebuke the devil over your other nine-tenths:

> *Bring all the tithes into the storehouse,*
> *That there may be food in My house,*
> *And try Me now in this,"*
> *Says the Lord of hosts,*
> *"If I will not open for you the windows of heaven*
> *And pour out for you such blessing*
> *That there will not be room enough to receive it.*
>
> *"And I will rebuke the devourer for your sakes . . .*
> *And all nations will call you blessed,*
> *For you will be a delightful land,"*
> *Says the Lord of hosts.* (Malachi 3:10-12, emphasis added)

Wow! When you tithe, God derails the devil's plan to eat up everything you've got. He turns the tables on the devil. It's as if He devours the devil's plans to steal the nine-tenths you have left. Otherwise, you have to rebuke Satan yourself. And that's a battle I want to avoid!

This passage also tells you how to tithe. Notice that it tells you to "bring all the tithes to the storehouse"—not half of it, all of it. We are to bring it to the storehouse. In the Old Testament, the storehouse referred to the treasury of the temple (see 1 Kings 7:51). For you, that's your local church. Many people think they can tithe to a televangelist or Bible teacher or even to a mission. But that's not what this means. You don't give your tithe to Marilyn Hickey Ministries or any other ministry. You sow it into your storehouse, the place you go to when you need help, prayer, encouragement, and fellowship. As much as I love my donors, whose offerings I am truly grateful for, Marilyn Hickey Ministries is not their church.

I studied to find out why God refers to Himself as the "Lord of hosts" in this passage. That's *Jehovah Sabaoth*, the Lord of hosts of all that He has created—in this case, hosts of angels. This is like saying that God is going to move on all kinds of hosts to get the money to you. He can send angels. They are ministering spirits for the household of faith (see Hebrews 1:14).

These angels say, "Hey, we have to get money to them. We have to see that they get blessed. They're tithers. They put God first. They brought their tithe into the storehouse." There are "hosts" of ways that God can open up the heavens and give you a blessing because the tithe belongs to Him. It's first fruit.

But let's not stop there; the best part of this passage is in verse 12: *"And all nations will call you blessed, . . . Says the Lord of hosts."* When you tithe, you will have the "what" to do the "why" as the Lord directs you, and you will be called "blessed" not just by God but by others. God blesses you so you can bless others!

If you put God first, the rest can fall in line. Pray about that and ask God to help you to put Him first. And if you aren't already, pray about becoming a tither—a committed, consistent tither. Just remember, when things go bad, or when you quit tithing, then you cut off what God can do because you're not putting the kingdom first. You're putting your money first.

Let me throw in a word to the young people—start early. You need to be tithing, and you need to be sowing offerings. Do you think you don't have enough money? My daughter, Sarah, started tithing when she was about eight or nine. She was cleaning out a hairdresser's combs, and she paid her a silver dollar; she tithed on that—10 cents. When she became a teenager, she received an allowance. I'm going to let Sarah tell you her testimony on tithing:

> "I kind of thought I would like to have more [money]. So, I started tithing on what I wanted to receive, but I didn't tell my parents. I just tithed on what I was believing God for. And probably within about four to six months, they upped my allowance to what I wanted God to give me— what I had been tithing."

I love that story. In fact, no matter what age you are, I want to pray with you that you would begin tithing now, if you don't already. Say:

> Father, I pray that you will help me set aside my fear and begin to tithe when I get paid or when any money comes my way. I pray that I will be encouraged to bring my tithe into my church—and do it joyfully! I expect the blessings that come with tithing and will see the devourer rebuked from the very moment I drop that tithe into the basket. Father, I pray that the nine-tenths that I live on

will stretch and will be sufficient to meet all my needs supernaturally. I pray that I will begin to experience the abundance that comes with putting your kingdom first, in Jesus's name. Amen!

Checkup! What's Wrong? – Negative Attitudes

God can heal anything, anything but a bad attitude. Only you can "heal" that! It's your choice. If you walk into church thinking, *Well, I know he's going to teach on tithing—they're going to ask for money again this morning . . .* Where will that get you? I doubt you're going to be very blessed because your attitude is so rotten.

As we already saw in 2 Corinthians 9:6-8, God loves cheerful givers. God doesn't want us to give grudgingly or because we *have* to. He wants us to give because we *want* to. I can assure you that it really works. I've been tithing since I was 11 years old—five years before I became a Christian. And you know, I've always found that tithing works. When I was in college, I was the only girl on campus who had a fur coat. When I finished college, I didn't owe a dime, though nobody helped me with my college tuition. I was a tither, and God took me through school miraculously. Don't tell me tithing doesn't work; it's too late!

This "how" is crucial because you must have the right attitude about money. To get rid of lack, you must get rid of lust. You cannot have a lust for money because it will not lead to biblical abundance. The Bible says, *"Ye ask, and receive not, because ye ask amiss, that ye may consume it upon your lusts"* (James 4:3 KJV). To be honest, I think we all experience this at times. Sometimes we just feel jealous of people who get good things. There are times when I have wanted things just for me.

Many years ago, shortly after we got married, my husband, Wally, gave the money we had been saving for a new car into an offering. I was so upset! I wanted that car! But Wally had the right attitude; I didn't. Fortunately, God honored Wally's sacrifice and ignored my grumbling. Shortly after that, John Osteen spoke at our church, and after he saw the word "car" over Wally's head, he raised an offering for us for our new car. I have since learned my lesson.

When people get new things, don't get jealous. That's foolishness, and it won't accomplish anything. Rather, it gets you into a wrong attitude and pattern of thinking. Instead, go hang around them. Maybe some of the faith they have will rub off on you. Say, "Would you like to pray for me?"

A Portuguese pastor I know has a big church in Portugal, with easily over 40,000 people. He also has a big church in Angola, with probably 50,000 in attendance. God has given him that nation. He has such a passion for the lost. But for years, he needed a really nice, big church building to bring all of his people in at one time for his services and conferences, so they built it.

He is an electrical engineer and also has a degree as an architect, so you can imagine what a beautiful building they built, a dream come true, right outside of Lisbon. It had the best of everything. In September of the same year it was finished, they were getting ready for a big conference, and I was to be there for it. Everything was ready to go. Five days before I got there, the government went in and said, "This building does not pass inspection, and we are tearing it down!" They brought bulldozers, and for a week, they ripped on that building until they took it to the ground.

When the news came to me, I asked him, "George, what did you do? Did you fall on the floor? Did you say, 'I'm just going to give up on God'? Did you backslide? Did you scream? Did you rebuke the devil? Did you say, 'God, do you hate me'?"

"No, Marilyn," he said, "I didn't. I told God that I had put the best into that building. I felt that He had me build that building. I asked Him, 'How did I miss it? How confused can I be?'"

Then God said, "Trust me, George. This is your first fruit. Now the next nine-tenths are going to come easy."

When George countered, "They ripped it up!" God replied, "I just took it as a sacrifice, as first fruit."

He said, "But God, if I'd known they were going to rip it up, I wouldn't have put all those good things in it; I may have even used inferior material."

"That's why I didn't tell you, because it had to be the best," God said and continued, "I'm going to bless you. You can't give your first fruit that I won't rebuke the devourer."

Well, the whole thing came to the attention of some kind of human rights group; they jumped on it, and they began to put pressure on the Portuguese government. The government finally succumbed and offered to pay him double for the building and give him more land because of the ugly thing they had done!

When we do what God tells us to do, He will rebuke the devourer! George didn't fall into the trap of negative attitudes. He stayed focused on the Lord and, instead of ranting and raving, turned to God to vent his disappointments and frustrations. His positive attitude and trust in God turned it around, and his sacrifice became a gift to God. Furthermore, he was compensated more than double! Isn't that just like God?

Jesus, of course, is our perfect role model to follow in terms of the right attitudes about money. You might say, "But I just have so little to give." Jesus knows how to take a little and make it a lot. One time, when He and Peter were in Capernaum, some of the temple tax collectors asked Peter if Jesus paid the temple tax. Think about this. Why should Jesus have to pay that or any tax for that matter? He could have said, "I don't owe any taxes. I own the whole place. Why should I pay taxes? I own it all." Instead, He instructed Peter, *"Go to the sea, cast in a hook, and take the fish that comes up first. And when you have opened its mouth, you will find a piece of money; take that and give it to them for Me and you"* (Matthew 17:27). Jesus took a little—actually, He started with nothing—and made it a lot. He can do the same for you.

In another instance, Jesus took a little boy's offering of just five loaves and two fish and fed over 5,000 people with it (see Matthew 14:13-21). You see, folks, when we go to Jesus, He can take a little and make it a lot. I'm telling you, Jesus knew God's plan of abundance, and He knew how to work it when He walked in the flesh.

If you follow what Jesus did and obey His precepts, you have opened the door for Him to come into your circumstances and make your "little" into a lot. If you will give a little and trust God, give thanks to God, and keep the right attitude, you just don't know what God will do for you!

Think about it. When the little boy brought those five loaves and two fish to Him, Jesus didn't panic and say, "Oh God, where are you? There are 5,000 men here, not counting women and children. We're all going to starve out here!" No! He said, "Thank you, Father, that you always hear me." How was His attitude? Did He have a cheerful attitude? Yes! Absolutely, yes! And what did God do? He multiplied it! If you follow His precepts, He can take your little and multiply it. That's the way He is.

Checkup! What's Wrong? – Poor Work Ethics

Another thing to look at is your work ethic. America was founded on the "Puritan work ethic." Puritans emphasized putting God first, which meant they valued everything else in relation to God. It is a "theological and sociological concept emphasizing diligence and hard work within the life of the Christian." Putting God first in your job is serving the Lord: *"And whatever you do, do it heartily, as to the Lord and not to men, knowing that from the Lord you will receive the reward of the inheritance; for you serve the Lord Christ"* (Colossians 3:23-24).

Serving God is paramount to all that we do or undertake—work and discipline included. Paul, in his letter to the Thessalonians, emphasized this "how":

> *But we urge you, brothers and sisters, that you excel* [in this matter] *more and more, and to make it your ambition to live quietly and peacefully, and to mind your own affairs and work with your hands, just as we directed you, so that you will behave properly toward outsiders* [exhibiting good character, personal integrity, and moral courage worthy of the respect of the outside world]*, and be dependent on no one and in need of nothing* [be self-supporting].
> (1 Thessalonians 4:10-12 AMP)

The Bible tells us God's plan of abundance includes work. This is a key "how" to fulfill this plan. You've already seen that you have to renew your mind, you have to be a tither, and you have to work! And not just work—you must be diligent in all your work because you are serving the Lord. This is true especially if you're in a secular job, where your work can become part of your witness. Paul even decreed that if anybody didn't work, he shouldn't eat either (see 2 Thessalonians 3:10).

Work is a part of life. When Adam lived in the garden of Eden, he was working. Even when you go to heaven, if you think you're going to sit on a pink cloud, eat chocolates, and play a harp, you're in for a rude awakening. You are not! Look at John; he was busy when he was caught up to heaven. He was working with the angel who was speaking with him and was measuring buildings and counting gemstones and more (see Revelation 21:14-21).

We must be diligent in all we do. How are you going to enjoy abundance if you're not diligent? You say, "Well, I tithe, and I give offerings." But you're sloppy in your work habits; you're not diligent. You get to work late. You leave early. You take long lunches. You steal pens and paper. You talk against the boss, and you listen to people who talk against the boss. Then you say, "I am going to be a millionaire." No, you're not. You're going to lose your job!

If you ask, "How come I'm not rich? How come my needs aren't met?" Is it because you're lazy and sloppy when God honors diligence? That's in the Bible! If you don't put in a good, honest day at work and you just slop along, or you say, "Well, I've given my notice so I can act any old way,"— then you could be cruising for a bruising! Jesus sees the way you are acting. Is that the way you want Him to act toward you? I don't believe you do.

In our culture today, the focus is not on how to be transformed to do a better job. Today's focus is on leisure. Prospective employees' questions focus on how much vacation time they will get. How much sick time? What are the holidays? It's not about how they can do a good job or excel in their work. It's a leisure attitude, and it's not biblical.

We must work diligently and go the extra mile—do things as unto the Lord. If you want to be rich, be diligent: *"He who has a slack hand becomes poor, but the hand of the diligent makes rich"* (Proverbs 10:4).

Jesus urges us to do more than what is required: *"And whoever compels you to go one mile, go with him two"* (Matthew 5:41). If you take on Jesus's attitude, that's when you really begin to see abundance in your life.

When I first started to travel (I think it was maybe the second church I ever went to), the pastor told me they would receive an offering for my ministry. I really needed it because he hadn't paid for my airline ticket, though he did pay for the place where I stayed. He received the offering, but when it was time to leave, he said, "Don't worry about it. I'll just send it to you."

I went home, but the offering didn't come. We called and told him we hadn't received the offering yet. He said, "Oh, not to worry, not to worry. I'll send it; you'll get it. Give me a week. I'll have it to you." Well, it didn't come. I was worried, so then we wrote, again telling him we hadn't received the offering yet. He wrote a letter back, again telling me the offering was on its way. It didn't come, and I was still worrying.

That's when God told me that what he did was wrong. He went on to say, "But if you'll go the second mile, I'll bless you beyond what you can imagine. Just give him the offering in your mind. It's not yours anymore. Just sow it as a seed in his ministry, and I'll bless your socks off because you'll have the right attitude. Go the second mile!" I went the second mile! And God has so blessed me when working with pastors that in over 40 years, that's the only really negative experience that I have had—and that's not really negative because God made it positive when my attitude got right.

I see that man occasionally, and when he sees me, he's so warm, and he's so friendly, and I'm so warm. You say, "You're pretending." I'm not. I have the victory. I went the second mile.

Checkup! What's Wrong? – Selfishness

Whether you have a little or a lot, don't be selfish. Generosity is yet another "how" in God's plan of abundance. I have found the more generous I am, the more generosity comes back to me. It is the truth. You can be a poor person yet be generous. Then watch God. You won't stay poor. You may not get a huge raise or suddenly inherit a fortune, but your bills will be paid, there will be food on your table, your car won't break down, and your other needs will be met.

Some people have a poverty attitude, and they are always going to hold onto it. They think I have to hold onto it. I have to squirrel it away. Folks, that's the way to keep the blessings of God from coming along. When you are able to meet a need, do it! This "how" of being generous often requires that you go the extra mile as well, but it's so rewarding.

As a cautionary word, those rewards of generosity can be thwarted if you don't heed Jesus's warning. When you give, don't give to be seen by men. Jesus said:

> *Take heed that you do not do your charitable deeds before*
> *men, to be seen by them. Otherwise you have no reward from*
> *your Father in heaven. Therefore, when you do a charitable*
> *deed, do not sound a trumpet before you as the hypocrites do*
> *in the synagogues and in the streets, that they may have glory*
> *from men. Assuredly, I say to you, they have their reward.*
> *But when you do a charitable deed, do not let your left hand*
> *know what your right hand is doing, that your charitable*
> *deed may be in secret; and your Father who sees in secret will*
> *Himself reward you openly.* (Matthew 6:1-4)

Generosity is between you and the Lord. It's so secret that your left hand doesn't know what your right hand is doing! You want to avoid the hypocrisy of the Pharisees who sought public approval and made all kinds of showy displays when they gave their offerings—blowing trumpets before them—really!?

Jesus didn't commend the rich who put a lot into the offering, but he commented favorably on the humble offering of a widow who only had two mites—all that she had—to put into the treasury (see Mark 12:41-44). Though the Bible doesn't say what happened to that poor widow, I bet she saw her needs met and was so blessed she even became more generous in her giving. Why do I think that? Because God said He would rebuke the devourer for her sake!

On the other hand, we read the story of the rich, young ruler in Matthew 19 and Mark 10. He came to Jesus asking Him what he should do to gain eternal life. Jesus told him to keep the commandments, to which he replied, *"Which ones?"* Interestingly, Jesus didn't answer with all the commandments. I would have thought that Jesus would have emphasized the ones pertaining to his relationship with God. Instead, He emphasized those pertaining to man's relationship with man:

> *Jesus said, "'You shall not murder,' 'You shall not commit adultery,' 'You shall not steal,' 'You shall not bear false witness,' 'Honor your father and your mother,' and, 'You shall love your neighbor as yourself.'"* (Matthew 19:18-19)

The young man responded that he had done all those things since his youth and pressed Jesus still further, asking, *"What do I still lack?"* I love Jesus's attitude toward this young man. He didn't get short with him or shrug him off. Instead, He responded to Him in love:

Then Jesus, looking at him, loved him, and said to him, "One thing you lack: Go your way, sell whatever you have and give to the poor, and you will have treasure in heaven; and come, take up the cross, and follow Me.

But he was sad at this word, and went away sorrowful, for he had great possessions." (Mark 10:20-22)

I think this is one of the saddest stories in the Bible. I believe that he really was seeking after eternal life, but when he counted the cost, it was too high. This young man encountered God face-to-face but couldn't let go of his earthly possessions in order to follow Jesus. Though he had great wealth, he couldn't let go of it to help the poor, his fellow man. I sometimes wonder what happened to him—what a contrast with the poor widow who gave all she had.

Checkup! What's Wrong? – The Words of Your Mouth

This "how" is where a lot of folks get hung up. They speak the problem and not the solution. When you're having a hard time financially, it's very difficult not to talk about it all the time because you think about it, you dream about it. But the Bible tells us that's very dangerous because when you start speaking the problem over and over again, you're not going to get the provision. God knows your problems. Guess what? God doesn't answer problems. He answers faith and responds to His promises.

Look at what Philippians 4:6-7 says:

Be anxious for nothing, but in everything by prayer and supplication, with thanksgiving, let your requests be made known to God; and the peace of God, which surpasses all understanding, will guard your hearts and minds through Christ Jesus.

If you will speak your request according to what God says and thank Him, it will keep you peaceful until you get the provision. James 1:26 adds: *"If anyone among you thinks he is religious, and does not bridle his tongue but deceives his own heart, this one's religion is useless."* Watch your mouth! "Useless" in this case means "vain, devoid of force, of no purpose."

If you start talking about your problem, you're making the solution void. You're voiding the thing that you want so much. Proverbs 6:2 says, *"You are snared by the words of your mouth; you are taken by the words of your mouth."* Furthermore, Proverbs 21:23 says, *"Whoever guards his mouth and tongue keeps his soul from troubles."* Don't speak the problem, which, if you think about it, is what the devil says. Rather, follow the advice of Hebrews 10:23: *"Let us hold fast the confession of our hope without wavering, for He who promised is faithful."*

When you don't see it, and it doesn't look good, keep saying what the Word says. When you don't see God's answer, keep saying what He says about it. Keep speaking the solution, the promise that the Word proclaims. Repeat it over and over again. And if you are asking, "How long do I keep this up?" Follow Caleb's example.

Joshua and Caleb knew they were supposed to inherit the promised land and were excited about that. Numbers 13 and 14 report what happened after Moses sent out 12 of the Israelites—including Joshua and Caleb—to explore the land that was to be given to them. Instead of a positive report, 10 of the spies made bad confessions and said the Israelites would never be able to conquer the giants living in the land. They spoke the problem and not the solution. As a result, the whole crowd had to wander in the wilderness for 40 years until the unbelieving generation died off. Only Joshua and Caleb reported what God said about the land, and only Joshua and Caleb received the promise.

If I had been Caleb, I could have murmured a lot against those murmurers in those 40 years. I could have said, "By the time we get there, I'll be 80 and won't even be able to enjoy what I get." But not Caleb! He believed God and rehearsed their future victory, maybe saying, "We've got the promised land. God fulfilled His promise of an abundant land, a land flowing with milk and honey!" When they finally got there, Caleb didn't say, "Oh, I'm too old." Rather he reminded Joshua of what God and Moses had promised him 45 years earlier:

> "Here I am this day, eighty-five years old. As yet I am as strong this day as on the day that Moses sent me; just as my strength was then, so now is my strength for war, both for going out and for coming in. Now therefore, give me this mountain of which the Lord spoke in that day; for you heard in that day how the Anakim were there, and that the cities were great and fortified. It may be that the Lord will be with me, and I shall be able to drive them out as the Lord said."
>
> And Joshua blessed him, and gave Hebron to Caleb the son of Jephunneh as an inheritance. (Joshua 14:10-13)

Caleb claimed the land he had walked on 45 years before he obtained it. He claimed his promise. Furthermore, he did exactly what he said he would do—he drove out three giants who were in the city of Hebron: "Caleb drove out the three sons of Anak from there: Sheshai, Ahiman, and Talmai, the children of Anak" (Joshua 15:14). He never considered his age; he confessed that he was just as strong at 85 as he was at 40. He got what he confessed.

If we don't say what the Lord says and instead follow the ways of the world, it is possible to end up like the Israelites did after they had been in the promised land. When they did what they saw the world around them doing despite the warnings of the prophets God sent to them, God had no other recourse but to deal with them according to the world's ways:

> *"Just as the Lord of hosts determined to do to us,*
> *According to our ways and according to our deeds,*
> *So He has dealt with us."* (Zechariah 1:6)

On the other hand, consider the widow of a prophet who died and had left debts behind that she was unable to pay. The creditor was going to take her two sons as slaves to satisfy the outstanding debt. When she cried out to Elisha, he told her to make use of what she did have—a jar of oil. Elisha instructed her to borrow a lot of empty oil containers from all her neighbors. Following his directions, she brought them home, shut the door behind her and her sons, and proceeded to pour the oil from her jar into her neighbors' jars. When they ran out of empty jars, the oil ran out as well. *"Then she came and told the man of God. And he said, 'Go, sell the oil and pay your debt; and you and your sons live on the rest'"* (2 Kings 4:7).

I would say that was a pretty dire situation. We don't read of her going to her neighbors and complaining about the problem. Instead, she trusted that Elisha, the man of God, would have the wisdom to guide her through those rough times. She followed his instructions, which were from the Lord, as evidenced by the miracle his words brought.

You may not be facing giants or a creditor who is threatening to take away your kids, but you may be facing a gigantic financial problem. Don't talk the problem. Guard the words of your mouth and make sure they line up with what the Word says. Take heart! Stay strong and stay in faith. Faith can retire giant debt. When you are faithful, God is faithful to make a provision for you, even when things seem impossible.

Checkup! What's Wrong? – Impatience

This last "how"—be patient—is a rough one. Do you like to get answers in 24 hours? I like it in 24 minutes! But I have to remember, *"By your patience possess your souls"* (Luke 21:19). We can't rush God, for He is bringing his purposes to pass. When you're believing for finances and believing for jobs or other sources of income, many times, it is a process.

I remember when I first started teaching on the radio. I thought that when I got on 10 radio stations, I would have arrived. Well, I got on 10—it took about a year. Then I thought, *What's 10? I want on 50.* It took me another year-and-a-half to get on 50. I learned a lesson. It seemed that as my faith grew, the process went faster. Within four years, I was on over 400 radio stations and had started on television—but it was a process, and it came with patience.

Patience also means that you don't give up: *"And let us not be weary in well doing: for in due season we shall reap, if we faint not"* (Galatians 6:9 KJV). It also means that you're not lazy: *"Do not become sluggish, but imitate those who through faith and patience inherit the promises"* (Hebrews 6:12). Faith and patience are twins.

There is often a delay between the promise and its fulfillment. For example, look at Abraham. Hebrews 6:15 tells us that *"after he had patiently endured, he obtained the promise."* Abraham was first promised descendants 25 years before Isaac, his son, was born. He was 75 when God told him He would make him a great nation (see Genesis 12:2), and Abraham was 100 when Isaac was born (see Genesis 21:5). The same is true for you; you need patience so that after you have done the will of God, you might receive the promise—it could be tomorrow, or it might take years.

My husband, Wally, was quite a gardener. Gardening takes a lot of patience! I noticed that he pulled weeds and put stuff in to keep weeds from gaining a foothold. As you know, weeds can absolutely choke out your garden. It takes a lot of patience and hard work, controlling the weeds and fertilizing and watering. Similarly, we must pull out the things that will keep us from hanging on until the end—until we obtain the promise. And we must feed our spirit with the truth. If somebody is speaking negative words to us, pull away from them! If you have negative thoughts, feed yourself the Word. Call in reinforcements. If you are feeling like this thing's going down the drain, call somebody and declare a faith confession, even if you don't feel like it at all. I've gotten some of my best healings when I felt the worst, but I called somebody. They would ask how I was, and I'd confess that I was the best I'd ever been in my life!

So how do you patiently wait for the promise? Pull out the weeds! Fertilize it with the Word! And water it with your positive confession.

I want to give you six affirmations for the next few days to help you to stand firm. Copy them and put them in your Bible or hang them on your bathroom mirror or someplace you are bound to see them.

Affirmation #1

Get up in the morning and say: "God has not given me a spirit of fear, but I have power. I have love, and I have a sound mind" (see 2 Timothy 1:7). Repeat it throughout the day as needed.

Affirmation #2

After you get up, say: "God teaches me to honor Him with my substance and the first fruit of all my increase. That means I'm going to increase and have plenty" (see Proverbs 3:9-10).

Affirmation #3

Repeat the following as needed throughout the day: "God is able today to make all grace abound toward me, that I always have all sufficiency in all things and have an abundance for every good work" (see 2 Corinthians 9:8).

Affirmation #4

Say: "The Lord will open to me his good treasure, the heavens, to give the rain to the land in its season, and to bless all the work of my hands. I will lend to many nations but will not borrow" (see Deuteronomy 28:12). I'm not going to be a debtor. I don't believe in debt; it's my great enemy.

Affirmation #5

Repeat: "I will trust in the Lord with all my heart. I will not depend on my own understanding. I will seek God's will in all I do, and He will direct my path" (see Proverbs 3:5-6). Why? Because you're transforming your mind with the Word.

Affirmation #6

Finally, confess that "I will lay up gold as dust, and the Almighty will be my defense, and I will have plenty of silver because God is my source" (see Job 22:24-25).

4

MILLIONAIRE FAITH

If you do a thorough study of Scripture, you will find that millionaire faith is paired with mega faith. When Jesus spoke to the Syrophoenician woman, He said she had great faith (see Matthew 15:28). It was actually millionaire faith. I want you to get a new vision of yourself, so you can believe that God does not want you to be poor. In reality, He wants you to be rich. He wants you to have millionaire status. Being a millionaire really is within reach of any Christian.

We have already seen that God promises abundance (the "what") over and over again to his people because He has a purpose (the "why") for it. It is not just for us to enjoy a really soft life. God has freely given us all things (see 2 Peter 1:3) with a purpose—to bless the kingdom and take the gospel to the world—and He even gives us guidelines on "how" to get them.

Hosea 4:6 says, *"My people are destroyed for lack of knowledge."* It doesn't say they perish for lack of faith. It says they perish for lack of knowledge.

Many times, we have faith, but we don't have the knowledge, and faith has to work in an environment of knowledge. We might say, "Well, I have faith to be a millionaire," but if you don't have the knowledge of "how" to be a millionaire, you may never be one.

Some Success Stories

Let me give you an example of a real success story. South Korea was a very poor country after the Korean War. The people who were in Dr. Yonggi Cho's church were very, very poor people. Following the war, they were hungry; few had enough to eat. Their country was in shambles. It was pitiful living there, but these Christians began to get a hold of the Word. Dr. Cho began to preach the Word to the blue-collar people who made up his congregation. They had praise and worship services. Some criticized him, saying that if he had worship and prayed for the sick, he wouldn't attract the white-collar people. (There were only a few white-collar people at the time.)

Dr. Cho didn't care what they said. He only cared about what God said, so he continued to have praise and worship. He continued to teach faith. He continued to pray for the sick. He proclaimed that doing so would make blue-collar people into white-collar, faithful, and faith-filled believers, and that is exactly what happened.

The last time I checked (well over 15 years ago), he had over 52,000 millionaires (and that doesn't count billionaires) in attendance! The naysayers have been proven wrong, and as always, the Word is true, and the gospel of Jesus Christ has spread throughout South Korea. Today, his Yoido Full Gospel Church has become a household name in South Korea. In fact, at one point, it was the largest church in the world, with a congregation of over 800,000 people.

Let me tell you another incident. I have a friend who pastors in Malaysia. Malaysia has become a more prosperous country in recent times, but Malaysia hasn't always been that way. It is primarily Muslim, with some Buddhists and a very small percentage of Christians. This pastor has a very strong church there, and his people really love to witness and win souls.

One of the men in his church was a doctor who witnessed to all of his patients. A Buddhist man who came to him was having a very hard time physically. He opened up and told the doctor that it wasn't just his physical health. He was also having trouble with his marriage, his finances, and his business.

The doctor began witnessing to him and finally, he got the Buddhist man to go to church with him. When he went to the service, he got saved. Now, of course, this doctor had been praying for him, and he was ripe. He got born again! It took his wife a little longer. She kept some idols around and hid them and prayed to them for about a year. But finally, she came clean and brought all the Buddhas out and smashed them! She really turned her life over to Jesus.

I have met this man and know him well. He isn't just a millionaire—he is a billionaire! At the time I heard this, he was the richest man in Malaysia. Two of his children are missionaries, his marriage is together, and his health is good.

You Can Be a Millionaire

It is not impossible for you to be a millionaire. You must get your thinking to the point where you don't think it's for somebody else in your church, family, or neighborhood—it's for you! You must believe that God wants you to fulfill His plan of abundance for your life, and He is for you. I want you to believe that you can be a millionaire.

It's a new beginning for you, but remember, it's going to take patience, and it's going to be a process. It's also going to take mega faith, holding onto and speaking the Word. It will take these principles in order to see it come to pass. It's easy to say, "Oh, I'm going to be a millionaire." It's harder to say, "I am a millionaire." But it is possible because "Nothing is impossible with God" (see Luke 1:37).

Your abundance starts with your faith, and faith works through love: *"For in Christ Jesus neither circumcision nor uncircumcision avails anything, but faith working through love"* (Galatians 5:6). Faith is also a gift of God:

> *For by grace you have been saved through faith, and that not of yourselves; it is the gift of God, ... For we are His workmanship, created in Christ Jesus for good works, which God prepared beforehand that we should walk in them.* (Ephesians 2:8-10)

Those good works include your giving. Not only should you give to God through your tithes, but God also wants you to give to the poor, for when you do, He will repay you: *"He who has pity on the poor lends to the Lord, and He will pay back what he has given"* (Proverbs 19:17).

God also encourages us to provide for the needs of other Christians: *". . . distributing to the needs of the saints, given to hospitality"* (Romans 12:13) and to support missionaries. When Jesus sent out his 12 disciples to begin to do ministry on their own, He told them: *"Provide neither gold nor silver nor copper in your money belts, nor bag for your journey, nor two tunics, nor sandals, nor staffs; for a worker is worthy of his food"* (Matthew 10:9-10).

As we discussed earlier, millionaire faith also requires that you first give yourself and be transformed:

> *I beseech you therefore, brethren, by the mercies of God, that you present your bodies a living sacrifice, holy, acceptable*

to God, which is your reasonable service. And do not be conformed to this world, but be transformed by the renewing of your mind, that you may prove what is that good and acceptable and perfect will of God. (Romans 12:1-2)

Presenting yourself to God means you are allowing the God of the universe, who only wants what is best for you, to use you to do the work of the kingdom as He wills. It is a sacrifice on your part, but the rewards are out of this world. When you follow His will and his commandments, you will be blessed:

Praise the Lord!

Blessed is the man who fears the Lord,
Who delights greatly in His commandments.

Wealth and riches will be in his house,
And his righteousness endures forever.
Unto the upright there arises light in the darkness;
He is gracious, and full of compassion, and righteous.
A good man deals graciously and lends;
He will guide his affairs with discretion.
Surely he will never be shaken;
The righteous will be in everlasting remembrance.

He has dispersed abroad,
He has given to the poor;
His righteousness endures forever;
His horn will be exalted with honor.
(Psalm 112:1, 3-6, 9)

This is a great passage! It reveals how the "What," "Why," and "How" work together in the life of a godly, righteous man. The *"wealth and riches will be in his house"* is the "what."

Verses 5 and 9 describe the "why": *"A good man deals graciously and lends . . . He has dispersed abroad, He has given to the poor."* This wealthy person not only graciously lends to those in need, but I believe he supports missionaries (dispersed abroad) and gives alms to the poor.

"How" he became wealthy is also detailed. He fears the Lord and delights in and obeys His commandments; he is gracious and full of compassion; and he guides his affairs with discretion and is not shaken. He believes what God says and stands firm in his faith. His attitude is in line with God's Word, and he is generous. It appears he is an honest and hard-working man, which may be how he gained his wealth. As a result, *"His righteousness endures forever"* (verse 9).

Biblical Guidelines for Financial Success

The following are some biblical guidelines to consider when you are beginning to think like a millionaire. Review them from time to time to check on your progress.

1. Be balanced. Scripture is balanced. Heresy is taking a truth out of balance. Jesus stuck to what was written.

   Then Jesus was led up by the Spirit into the wilderness to be tempted by the devil. And when He had fasted forty days and forty nights, afterward He was hungry. Now when the tempter came to Him, he said, "If You are the Son of God, command that these stones become bread."

   But He answered and said, "It is written, 'Man shall not live by bread alone, but by every word that proceeds from the mouth of God.'"

Then the devil took Him up into the holy city, set Him on the pinnacle of the temple, and said to Him, "If You are the Son of God, throw Yourself down. For it is written:

'He shall give His angels charge over you,' and, 'In their hands they shall bear you up, Lest you dash your foot against a stone.'"

Jesus said to him, "It is written again, 'You shall not tempt the Lord your God.'"

Again, the devil took Him up on an exceedingly high mountain, and showed Him all the kingdoms of the world and their glory. And he said to Him, "All these things I will give You if You will fall down and worship me."

Then Jesus said to him, "Away with you, Satan! For it is written, 'You shall worship the Lord your God, and Him only you shall serve.'"

Then the devil left Him, and behold, angels came and ministered to Him. (Matthew 4:1-11)

2. Be willing to be blessed. *"But Jesus looked at them and said to them, 'With men this is impossible, but with God all things are possible'"* (Matthew 19:26).

3. Understand that promises are conditional. *"If you are willing and obedient, you shall eat the good of the land"* (Isaiah 1:19).

4. Never borrow money for depreciating items. *"The rich rules over the poor, and the borrower is servant to the lender"* (Proverbs 22:7).

5. Don't be security for another.

   Do not be one of those who shakes hands in a pledge,
   One of those who is surety for debts;
   If you have nothing with which to pay,
   Why should he take away your bed from under you?
   (Proverbs 22:26-27)

6. Be generous to the poor. *"He who has pity on the poor lends to the Lord; and He will pay back what he has given"* (Proverbs 19:17).

7. Don't give to the rich. *"He who oppresses the poor to increase his riches, and he who gives to the rich, will surely come to poverty"* (Proverbs 22:16).

8. Pay all debts on time. *"Do not withhold good from those to whom it is due, when it is in the power of your hand to do so"* (Proverbs 3:27).

9. Transfer ownership to God. *"Commit your works to the Lord, and your thoughts will be established"* (Proverbs 16:3).

10. Be diligent. *"He who has a slack hand becomes poor, but the hand of the diligent makes rich"* (Proverbs 10:4).

11. Learn to pray. *"The sacrifice of the wicked is an abomination to the Lord, but the prayer of the upright is His delight"* (Proverbs 15:8).

12. Plant abundantly. *"Honor the Lord with your possessions, and with the firstfruits of all your increase"* (Proverbs 3:9).

13. Learn to rule yourself. *"Whoever has no rule over his own spirit is like a city broken down, without walls"* (Proverbs 25:28).

14. Start talking like a winner.
    "A man's stomach shall be satisfied from the fruit of his mouth;
    From the produce of his lips he shall be filled.

Death and life are in the power of the tongue,
And those who love it will eat its fruit" (Proverbs 18:20-21).

15. Don't waste time on vengeance. *"Do not say, 'I will recompense evil';*
wait for the Lord, and He will save you" (Proverbs 20:22).

16. Invest first. *"Prepare your outside work, make it fit for yourself in the*
field; and afterward build your house" (Proverbs 24:27).

17. Diversify. *"Give a serving to seven, and also to eight, for you do not*
know what evil will be on the earth" (Ecclesiastes 11:2).

18. Get all the facts. *"He who answers a matter before he hears it, it is*
folly and shame to him" (Proverbs 18:13).

19. Seek God's righteous rather than trusting in wealth. *"Riches do not*
profit in the day of wrath, but righteousness delivers from death"
(Proverbs 11:4).

20. Go the extra mile. *"And whoever compels you to go one mile, go with*
him two" (Matthew 5:41).

21. Avoid get-rich-quick schemes. *"Hell and Destruction are never full;*
so the eyes of man are never satisfied" (Proverbs 27:20).

22. Don't expect to work for nothing.

Who ever goes to war at his own expense? Who plants
a vineyard and does not eat of its fruit? Or who tends a
flock and does not drink of the milk of the flock?

Do I say these things as a mere man? Or does not the law
say the same also? For it is written in the law of Moses,
"You shall not muzzle an ox while it treads out the grain." Is it

oxen God is concerned about? Or does He say it altogether for our sakes? For our sakes, no doubt, this is written, that he who plows should plow in hope, and he who threshes in hope should be partaker of his hope. If we have sown spiritual things for you, is it a great thing if we reap your material things? If others are partakers of this right over you, are we not even more?

Nevertheless we have not used this right, but endure all things lest we hinder the gospel of Christ. (1 Corinthians 9:7-12)

23. Select business partners with care. *"Confidence in an unfaithful man in time of trouble is like a bad tooth and a foot out of joint"* (Proverbs 25:19).

24. Just because it gets tough does not mean God is not working in your life. *"Where no oxen are, the trough is clean; but much increase comes by the strength of an ox"* (Proverbs14:4). Also, *"Most assuredly, I say to you, unless a grain of wheat falls into the ground and dies, it remains alone; but if it dies, it produces much grain"* (John 12:24).

Let's pray together. Say,

"God, I believe you want me to flourish. There is no question. It is in the Word, and I believe what the Bible says. I don't believe it was written for everybody else. It was written for me, too. I believe you are giving me a measure of faith that's going to make me a millionaire so that I can be a millionaire giver. My coming increase has a purpose to promote your kingdom. Now, give me hearing ears and seeing eyes to receive what I'm to receive in order to make this happen. In Jesus's name. Amen!"

5

SUPER ABUNDANCE

Look at 3 John v. 2 again: *"Beloved, I pray that you may prosper in all things and be in health, just as your soul prospers."* Blessings make you rich, but if you don't get your mind transformed about the "why" of money, you're going to be conformed to the world—and the "what" is going to hurt you rather than bless you. The things that you want so desperately are probably not going to come your way or they will come but have wings and fly away.

Now look at Mark 10:24-25: *"Children, how hard it is for those who trust in riches to enter the kingdom of God. It is easier for a camel to go through the eye of a needle than for a rich man to enter the kingdom of God."* Let me assure you, God is not against rich people because Job was rich. Abraham was rich; Isaac, Jacob, Solomon, David, Esther—they were all rich people.

The "camel and eye-of-the-needle" thing has always intrigued me. I understand that the "Eye of the Needle" was a little gateway that was opened by a gatekeeper only at night. People who were too late to go through the big gate (they locked the city gates to keep the city safe at night) used this little gate to get into the city. But if somebody were really late, they would be so sorry. If they had their camels laden with cargo, in order to go through the "needle," they would have to first unload the cargo the camel bore. Then the camel would have to get way down and they would have to lead the camel through that little, tiny gate. When they got it through the gate, then they'd go back and get all of their goods and put it back on the camel's back. Then they could go about their business.

How does that apply to you and me? What do we have to do? We have to take all this materialism and leave it at the gate. "Oh, God, I just have to have a BMW." No, leave it there. "Oh God, I just have to have a three-story house." No, leave it there. "Oh God, I just have to have a rich husband." No, leave it there. (He might be ugly and mean.) Just leave it all there and say, "The number-one thing I must have is Jesus." Then you can go through the narrow gate and when you get through it, He has unimaginable blessings waiting for you on the other side. God's plan for abundance starts and ends with Jesus. Jesus is your all-in-all. That is super abundance!

The problem is not "what" you have. The problem is "what" has you. Jesus said the problem was when people trust in riches. The reason some don't want to tithe is that they trust in their money more than they trust God to take care of them. The reason they don't want to sow offerings or alms is they believe they will never see it again. But if they trusted God, they would know that when they sow it, they would get it back and that God can even multiply it.

Trusting God means getting transformed from the world's thinking of "get all you can and can all you get." God's way is "Get all you can and give away all you can." Then watch God take you from little to much. As we just saw, Jesus said it's easier for a camel to go through the eye of a needle than for a rich man to enter the kingdom. When the disciples heard that, they were "greatly astonished," and wondered who could be saved. Jesus's response speaks volumes: *"With men it is impossible, but not with God; for with God all things are possible"* (Mark 10:27).

God can change people's attitudes toward money and ministry. Remember, we have to watch our attitude for it is a key to thriving and paying off debt. Hold on to your faith attitude, even when your situation doesn't look good, and time is almost up. Be transformed by God's Word and do what He tells you to do. Suddenly, you will have the breakthrough that you need.

I urge you to believe that God can change your thinking about money. Don't trust in money. Trust God. When you believe, when you obey his Word, when you put the kingdom first, you can go from just barely squeaking by to super abundance! It's possible because God is the God of the impossible!

It's important to remember that while our provision is on earth, our treasure is in heaven:

> Do not lay up for yourselves treasures on earth, where moth
> and rust destroy and where thieves break in and steal; but
> lay up for yourselves treasures in heaven, where neither moth
> nor rust destroys and where thieves do not break in and steal.
> (Matthew 6:19-20)

This means putting God first. It's hard because we trust these things that we have—and then to take them all off and leave them behind . . . ? But, oh, do you trust Jesus more? Only He can bring you through into eternal life and He will do such wonderful things for you in this life! I want you to really get into faith concerning material possessions. Money is not everything. God is everything. He is your source.

Now let's see if that's scriptural. Look at the rest of Mark 10, verse 29-30.

> So Jesus answered and said, "Assuredly, I say to you, there is no one who has left house or brothers or sisters or father or mother or wife or children or lands, for My sake and the gospel's, who shall not receive a hundredfold now in this time—houses and brothers and sisters and mothers and children and lands, with persecutions—and in the age to come, eternal life."

What did Jesus say you are supposed to get? "Houses, brothers, sisters, mothers, children, lands; with persecution and in the age to come, eternal life," right? Does God want to give you houses, lands, mothers, brothers, sisters? You'd better believe it because that's what He said—and God never lies.

You see, there are different levels of abundance, just like there are levels of faith and levels of glory. You go from faith to faith, glory to glory, and you can go from little to much. It works through faith and obedience to the Word of God and doing what He calls you to do—putting the kingdom first.

Will you put God and His kingdom first?

END NOTES

Page 14. World wealth and population: Wikipedia. "Distribution of Wealth by Country," accessed March 22, 2021: https://en.wikipedia.org/wiki/Distribution_of_wealth_by_country.

Page 29. Meaning of "Study" in 2 Timothy 2:15: Strong, James. Strong's Exhaustive Concordance Complete and Unabridged, s.v. "spoudázō." (Grand Rapids: Baker Book House, 1980).

Page 34. Storehouse as the treasury of the temple: Strong, James. Strong's Exhaustive Concordance Complete and Unabridged, s.v. "ôwtsâr." (Grand Rapids: Baker Book House, 1980). See also: Gesenius' Hebrew-Chaldee Lexicon

Page 34. Jehovah Sabaoth: Strong, James. Strong's Exhaustive Concordance Complete and Unabridged, s.v. "tsâbâ'." (Grand Rapids: Baker Book House, 1980).

Page 40. Puritan work ethic: Study.com. "Puritan Work Ethic: Definition & Overview" by Nate Sullivan, accessed March 22, 2021: https://study.com/academy/lesson/puritan-work-ethic-definition-lesson-quiz.html.

Page 46. Meaning of "Useless" in James 1:26: Strong, James. Strong's Exhaustive Concordance Complete and Unabridged, s.v. "tsâbâ'." (Grand Rapids: Baker Book House, 1980).

Page 54. Yoido Full Gospel Church attendance statistics: Leadership Network, accessed March 22, 2021: http://leadnet.org/world/.

ABOUT MARILYN HICKEY

Encouraging, optimistic, always upbeat and energetic even in her later years, Marilyn Hickey actively ministers internationally. As founder and president of *Marilyn Hickey Ministries*, a non-profit ministry and humanitarian organization based in Denver, Colorado, Marilyn has impacted many countries worldwide; from disaster relief efforts in Haiti, Indonesia, and Pakistan to providing food for the hungry in Mexico, Costa Rica, Russia, and the Philippines.

Her legacy includes significant visits to Islamic countries. In 2016, over one million people attended her healing meeting in Karachi, Pakistan.

Marilyn has had audiences with government leaders and heads of state all over the world. She was the first woman to join the board of directors for Dr. David Yonggi Cho (founder of the world's largest congregation, Yoido Full Gospel Church in South Korea). She has traveled to over 135 countries and plans to visit more in the years to come.

Along with her daughter, pastor Sarah Bowling, she co-hosts the daily television program, *Today with Marilyn & Sarah*, which is broadcasted globally. *Today with Marilyn & Sarah* is shown in nearly 200 countries with a potential viewing audience of 2.5 billion households worldwide. Marilyn has also authored over 100 publications.

She and her late husband, Wallace, were married over 50 years and have two children and four grandchildren. Marilyn holds the following degrees of education: Bachelor of Arts in Collective Foreign Languages from the University of Northern Colorado and an Honorary Doctorate of Divinity from Oral Roberts University.

In 2015, Marilyn was honored at Oral Roberts University with the prestigious Lifetime Global Achievement Award. This award recognizes individuals, or organizations, that have made a significant impact in the history of ORU and in the world. In 2019, Marilyn received an International Lifetime Peace Award from the Grand Imam and President of Pakistan.

In 2021, Marilyn was honored with two awards from the Assemblies of God Theological Seminary: The Pillar of Faith Award in acknowledgment of her worldwide impact on the Church through biblical teaching and sustainable healing ministry; and the Smith Wigglesworth Award given on behalf of the entire Assemblies of God fellowship in acknowledgment of her decades of service worldwide.

Marilyn's greatest passion and desire is to continue being a bridge-builder in countries around the world, and she shows no signs of stopping.

RECEIVE JESUS CHRIST AS LORD
AND SAVIOR OF YOUR LIFE

The first step to defeating Satan is to ask Jesus into your life. You can have His joy, peace, protection, and provision in your life starting today. You can know for sure that you will have life after death in heaven.

The Good News is that God sent Jesus Christ to be the Savior of the world. 1 Timothy 2:5-6 says, "For there is one God and one Mediator between God and men, the Man Christ Jesus, who gave Himself as ransom for all."

The Bible tells us how we can receive Jesus as Savior:

> *If you confess with your mouth the Lord Jesus and believe in your heart that God has raised Him from the dead, you will be saved. For with the heart one believes unto righteousness, and with the mouth confession is made unto salvation.* (Romans 10:9-10)

Would you like to begin a personal relationship with God and Jesus right now? You can! Simply pray this prayer in sincerity:

> Heavenly Father, I acknowledge that I need Your help. I am not able to change my life or circumstances through my own efforts. I know that I have made some wrong decisions in my life, and at this moment I turn away from those ways of thinking and acting. I believe You have provided a way for me through Jesus to receive Your blessings and help in my life. Right now, I believe and confess Jesus as my Lord and Savior. I ask Jesus

to come into my heart and give me a new life, by Your Spirit. I thank You for saving me and I ask for Your grace and mercy in my life. I pray this in Jesus's name.

If you just prayed to make Jesus your Lord, we want to know! Please call us today—toll free—at 888-637-4545. We will pray for you and send you a special gift to help you in your new life with Christ.

God's Plan
for
Abundance

What? Why? How?

Jesus came to give us an abundant life. In fact, abundance is God's will for us. But what does that abundant life look like? Scripture gives us insight into how His redemption not only provides for your salvation but also provides for all your needs—from finances to health. Third John 2 says, *"Beloved, I pray that you may prosper in all things and be in health, just as your soul prospers."* Beginning with the salvation of your soul, God's plan for abundance will begin to unfold in your life as you follow His kingdom principles for prosperous living.

Full of biblical examples, guidelines, and affirmations, *God's Plan for Abundance* will give you the what, why, and how of God's strategy for blessing you so that you can bless others.

Marilyn Hickey founded *Marilyn Hickey Ministries* more than 45 years ago with God's vision to cover the earth with the Word. This global miracle ministry has taken the gospel of salvation and the healing power of God to millions of people in over 130 nations. As one of the most respected and anointed Bible teachers worldwide, Marilyn has a unique and powerful ability to communicate deep biblical truths in a way that is understandable and practical for everyday life.

Marilyn & Sarah
MARILYN HICKEY MINISTRIES

PO Box 6598 • Englewood, CO 80155-6598